R

D0937666

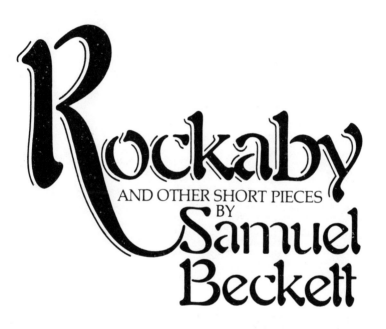

Rockaby

AND OTHER SHORT PIECES
BY
Samuel Beckett

Grove Press, Inc., New York

First Hardcover Edition 1981
First Printing 1981
ISBN: 0-394-51953-1
Grove Press ISBN: 0-8021-0209-3
Library of Congress Catalog Card Number: 80-8916

First Evergreen Paperbound Edition 1981
First Printing 1981
ISBN: 0-394-17924-2
Grove Press ISBN: 0-8021-4350-4
Library of Congress Catalog Card Number: 80-8916

Manufactured in the United States of America

Distributed by Random House, Inc., New York

GROVE PRESS, INC., 196 West Houston Street, New York, N.Y. 10014

Rockaby

Rockaby was first performed at the Center
for Theatre Research in Buffalo, in
association with the State University
of New York at Buffalo, on April 8, 1981.
It was directed by Alan Schneider and
produced by Daniel Labeille.

Woman and Voice . . . . . . Billie Whitelaw

W = *Woman in chair.*
V = *Her recorded voice.*

Fade up on W *in rocking chair
facing front downstage slightly
off centre audience left.*

Long pause.

W: More.

Pause. Rock and voice together.

V: till in the end
the day came
in the end came
close of a long day
when she said
to herself
whom else
time she stopped
time she stopped
going to and fro
all eyes
all sides

high and low
for another
another like herself
another creature like herself
a little like
going to and fro
all eyes
all sides
high and low
for another
till in the end
close of a long day
to herself
whom else
time she stopped
time she stopped
going to and fro
all eyes
all sides
high and low
for another
another living soul
one other living soul
going to and fro
all eyes like herself

all sides
high and low
for another
another like herself
a little like
going to and fro
till in the end
close of a long day
to herself
whom else
time she stopped
going to and fro
time she stopped
time she stopped

Together: echo of "time she
stopped," coming to rest of rock,
faint fade of light.

Long pause.

W: More.

Pause. Rock and voice together.

V: so in the end
    close of a long day
    went back in
    in the end went back in
    saying to herself
    whom else
    time she stopped
    time she stopped
    going to and fro
    time she went and sat
    at her window
    quiet at her window
    facing other windows
    so in the end
    close of a long day
    in the end went and sat
    went back in and sat
    at her window
    let up the blind and sat
    quiet at her window
    only window
    facing other windows
    other only windows
    all eyes
    all sides

high and low
for another
at her window
another like herself
a little like
another living soul
one other living soul
at her window
gone in like herself
gone back in
in the end
close of a long day
saying to herself
whom else
time she stopped
time she stopped
going to and fro
time she went and sat
at her window
quiet at her window
only window
facing other windows
other only windows
all eyes
all sides

high and low
for another
another like herself
a little like
another living soul
one other living soul

*Together: echo of "living soul,"
coming to rest of rock, faint
fade of light.*

Long pause.

W: More.

Pause. Rock and voice together.

V: till in the end
the day came
in the end came
close of a long day
sitting at her window
quiet at her window
only window

facing other windows
other only windows
all blinds down
never one up
hers alone up
till the day came
in the end came
close of a long day
sitting at her window
quiet at her window
all eyes
all sides
high and low
for a blind up
one blind up
no more
never mind a face
behind the pane
famished eyes
like hers
to see
be seen
no
a blind up
like hers

a little like
one blind up no more
another creature there
somewhere there
behind the pane
another living soul
one other living soul
till the day came
in the end came
close of a long day
when she said
to herself
whom else
time she stopped
time she stopped
sitting at her window
quiet at her window
only window
facing other windows
other only windows
all eyes
all sides
high and low
time she stopped
time she stopped

*Together: echo of "time she
stopped," coming to rest of rock,
faint fade of light.*

Long pause.

W: More.

Pause. Rock and voice together.

V: so in the end
close of a long day
went down
in the end went down
down the steep stair
let down the blind and down
right down
into the old rocker
mother rocker
where mother sat
all the years
all in black
best black
sat and rocked
rocked

till her end came
in the end came
off her head they said
gone off her head
but harmless
no harm in her
dead one day
no
night
dead one night
in the rocker
in her best black
head fallen
and the rocker rocking
rocking away
so in the end
close of a long day
went down
in the end went down
down the steep stair
let down the blind and down
right down
into the old rocker
those arms at last
and rocked

rocked
with closed eyes
closing eyes
she so long all eyes
famished eyes
all sides
high and low
to and fro
at her window
to see
be seen
till in the end
close of a long day
to herself
whom else
time she stopped
let down the blind and stopped
time she went down
down the steep stair
time she went right down
was her own other
own other living soul
so in the end
close of a long day
went down

down the steep stair
let down the blind and down
right down
into the old rocker
and rocked
rocked
saying to herself
no
done with that
the rocker
those arms at last
saying to the rocker
rock her off
stop her eyes
fuck life
stop her eyes
rock her off
rock her off

Together: echo of "rock her off,"
coming to rest of rock, slow
fade out.

NOTES

Light

Subdued on chair. Rest of stage dark.
Subdued spot on face constant through-
out, unaffected by successive fades.
Either wide enough to include narrow
limits of rock or concentrated on face
when still or at mid-rock. Then through-
out speech face slightly swaying in and
out of light.
Opening fade-up: first spot on face alone.
Long pause. Then light on chair.
Final fade-out: first chair. Long pause
with spot on face alone. Head slowly
sinks, comes to rest. Fade out spot.

W

Prematurely old. Unkempt grey hair.
Huge eyes in white expressionless face.
White hands holding ends of armrests.

Eyes

Now closed, now open in unblinking

gaze. About equal proportions section 1, increasingly closed 2 and 3, closed for good halfway through 4.

Costume

Black lacy high-necked evening gown. Long sleeves. Jet sequins to glitter when rocking. Incongruous frivolous head-dress set askew with extravagant trimmings to catch light when rocking.

Attitude

Completely still till fade-out of chair. Then in light of spot head slowly inclined.

Chair

Pale wood highly polished to gleam when rocking. Footrest. Vertical back. Rounded inward curving arms to suggest embrace.

Rock

Slight. Slow. Controlled mechanically without assistance from W.

Voice

Lines in italics spoken by W with V a
little softer each time.
W's "More" a little softer each time.
Towards end of section 4, say from "saying to herself" on, voice gradually softer.

Ohio Impromptu

Ohio Impromptu was first performed in the Drake Union, Stadium 2 Theater, in association with Ohio State University, on May 9, 1981. It was directed by Alan Schneider.

L = *Listener.*
R = *Reader.*
As alike in appearance as possible.

*Light on table midstage. Rest of stage in
darkness.*
Plain white deal table, say 8′ x 4′.
Two plain armless white deal chairs.

L *seated at table facing front towards end of
long side audience right. Bowed head propped
on right hand. Face hidden. Left hand on table.
Long black coat. Long white hair.*

R *seated at table in profile centre of short side
audience right. Bowed head propped on right
hand. Left hand on table. Book on table before
him open at last pages. Long black coat. Long
white hair.*

Black wide-brimmed hat at centre of table.

Fade up.

Ten seconds.

R *turns page.*

Pause.

R *(reading):* Little is left to tell. In a last—

L *knocks with left hand on table.*

Little is left to tell.

Pause. Knock.

In a last attempt to obtain relief he moved from where they had been so long together to a single room on the far bank. From its single window he could see the downstream extremity of the Isle of Swans.

Pause.

Relief he had hoped would flow from un-
familiarity. Unfamiliar room. Unfamiliar
scene. Out to where nothing ever shared.
Back to where nothing ever shared. From
this he had once half hoped some measure of relief might flow.

Pause.

Day after day he could be seen slowly
pacing the islet. Hour after hour. In his
long black coat no matter what the
weather and old world Latin Quarter hat.
At the tip he would always pause to
dwell on the receding stream. How in
joyous eddies its two arms conflowed and
flowed united on. Then turn and his slow
steps retrace.

Pause.

In his dreams—

Knock.

Then turn and his slow steps retrace.

Pause. Knock.

In his dreams he had been warned against this change. Seen the dear face and heard the unspoken words, Stay where we were so long alone together, my shade will comfort you.

Pause.

Could he not—

Knock.

Seen the dear face and heard the unspoken words, Stay where we were so long alone together, my shade will comfort you.

Pause. Knock.

Could he not now turn back? Acknowledge his error and return to where they were once so long alone together. Alone together so much shared. No. What he had done alone could not be undone. Nothing he had ever done alone could ever be undone. By him alone.

Pause.

In this extremity his old terror of night laid hold on him again. After so long a lapse that as if never been. *(Pause. Looks closer.)* Yes, after so long a lapse that as if never been. Now with redoubled force the fearful symptoms described at length page forty paragraph four. *(Starts to turn back the pages. Checked by L's left hand. Resumes relinquished page.)* White nights now again his portion. As when his heart was young. No sleep no braving sleep till— *(turns page)*—dawn of day.

Pause.

Little is left to tell. One night—

Knock.

Little is left to tell.

Pause. Knock.

One night as he sat trembling head in hands from head to foot a man appeared to him and said, I have been sent by—and here he named the dear name—to comfort you. Then drawing a worn volume from the pocket of his long black coat he sat and read till dawn. Then disappeared without a word.

Pause.

Some time later he appeared again at the same hour with the same volume and this time without preamble sat and read it through again the long night through. Then disappeared without a word.

Pause.

So from time to time unheralded he would appear to read the sad tale through again and the long night away. Then disappear without a word.

Pause.

With never a word exchanged they grew
to be as one.

Pause.

Till the night came at last when having
closed the book and dawn at hand he did
not disappear but sat on without a word.

Pause.

Finally he said, I have had word from—
and here he named the dear name—that I
shall not come again. I saw the dear face
and heard the unspoken words, No need
to go to him again, even were it in your
power.

Pause.

So the sad—

Knock.

Saw the dear face and heard the unspoken words, No need to go to him
again, even were it in your power.

Pause. Knock.

So the sad tale a last time told they sat on
as though turned to stone. Through the
single window dawn shed no light. From
the street no sound of reawakening. Or
was it that buried in who knows what
thoughts they paid no heed? To light of
day. To sound of reawakening. What
thoughts who knows. Thoughts, no, not
thoughts. Profounds of mind. Buried in
who knows what profounds of mind. Of
mindlessness. Whither no light can
reach. No sound. So sat on as though
turned to stone. The sad tale a last time
told.

Pause.

Nothing is left to tell.

Pause. R makes to close book.

Knock. Book half-closed.

Nothing is left to tell.

Pause. R closes book.

Knock.

Silence. Five seconds.

Simultaneously they lower their right hands to table, raise their heads and look at each other. Unblinking. Expressionless.

Ten seconds.

Fade out.

All
Strange
Away

Imagination dead imagine. A place, that again. Never another question. A place, then someone in it, that again. Crawl out of the frowsy deathbed and drag it to a place to die in. Out of the door and down the road in the old hat and coat like after the war, no, not that again. Five foot square, six high, no way in, none out, try for him there. Stool, bare walls when the light comes on, women's faces on the walls when the light comes on. In a corner when the light comes on tattered syntaxes of Jolly and Draeger Praeger Draeger, all right. Light off and let him be, on the stool, talking to himself in the last person, murmuring, no sound, Now where is he, no, Now he is here. Sitting, standing, walking, kneeling, crawling, lying, creeping, in the dark and in the light, try all. Imagine light. Imagine light. No visible source, glare at full, spread all over, no shadow, all six planes shining the same, slow on, ten seconds on earth to full, same off, try that. Still his crown touches the ceiling, moving not,

say a lifetime of walking bowed and full
height when brought to a stand. It goes
out, no matter, start again, another place,
someone in it, keep glaring, never see,
never find, no end, no matter. He says, no
sound, The longer he lives and so the
further goes the smaller they grow, the
reasoning being the fuller he fills the
space and so on, and the emptier, same
reasoning. Hell this light from nothing no
reason any moment, take off his coat, no,
naked, all right, leave it for the moment.
Sheets of black paper, stick them to the
wall with cobweb and spittle, no good,
shine like the rest. Imagine what needed,
no more, any given moment, needed no
more, gone, never was. Light flows, eyes
close, stay closed till it ebbs, no, can't do
that, eyes stay open, all right, look at that
later. Black bag over his head, no good,
all the rest still in light, front, sides, back,
between the legs. Black shroud, start
search for pins. Light on, down on knees,
sights pin, makes for it, light out, gets pin
in dark, light on, sights another, light out,

so on, years of time on earth. Back on the
stool in the shroud saying, That's better,
now he's better, and so sits and never
stirs, clutching it to him where it gapes,
till it all perishes and rots off of him and
hangs off of him in black flitters. Light
out, long dark, candle and matches,
imagine them, strike one to light, light
on, blow out, light out, strike another,
light on, so on. Light out, strike one to
light, light on, light all the same, can-
dlelight in light, blow out, light out, so
on. No candle, no matches, no need,
never were. As he was, in the dark any
length, then the light when it flows till it
ebbs any length, then again, so on, sitting, standing, walking, kneeling, crawling, lying, creeping, all any length, no
paper, no pins, no candle, no matches,
never were, talking to himself no sound
in the last person any length, five foot
square, six high, all white when light at
full, no way in, none out. Falling on his
knees in the dark to murmur, no sound,
Fancy is his only hope. Surprised by light

in this posture, hope and fancy on his
lips, crawling lifelong habit to a corner
here shadowless and similarly sinking
head to ground here shining back into his
eyes. Imagine eyes burnt ashen blue and
lashes gone, lifetime of unseeing glaring,
jammed open, one lightning wince per
minute on earth, try that. Have him say,
no sound, No way in, none out, he's not
here. Tighten it round him, three foot
square, five high, no stool, no sitting, no
kneeling, no lying, just room to stand and
revolve, light as before, faces as before,
syntaxes upended in opposite corners.
The back of his head touches the ceiling,
say a lifetime of standing bowed. Call
floor angles deasil a, b, c and d and ceiling likewise e, f, g and h, say Jolly at b
and Draeger at d, lean him for rest with
feet at a and head at g, in dark and light,
eyes glaring, murmuring, He's not here,
no sound, Fancy is his only hope. Physique, flesh and fell, nail him to that
while still tender, nothing clear, place
again. Light as before, all white still when

at full, flaking plaster or the like, floor
like bleached dirt, aha. Faces now naked
bodies, eye level, two per wall, eight in
all, all right, details later. All six planes
hot when shining, aha. So dark and cold
any length, shivering more or less, feeble
slaps want of room at all flesh within
reach, little stamps of hampered feet, so
on. Same system light and heat with
sweat more or less, cringing away from
walls, burning soles, now one, now the
other. Murmur unaffected, He's not here,
no sound, Fancy dead, gaping eyes unaffected. See how light stops at five soft
and mild for bodies, eight no more, one
per wall, four in all, say all of Emma. First
face alone, lovely beyond words, leave it
at that, then deasil breasts alone, then
thighs and cunt alone, then arse and hole
alone, all lovely beyond words. See how
he crouches down and back to see, back
of head against face when eyes on cunt,
against breasts when on hole, and vice
versa, all most clear. So in this soft and
mild, crouched down and back with

hands on knees to hold himself together, say deasil first from face through hole then back through face, murmuring, Imagine him kissing, caressing, licking, sucking, fucking and buggering all this stuff, no sound. Then halt and up to position of rest, back of head touching the ceiling, gaze on ground, lifetime of unbloody bowed unseeing glaring. Imagine lifetime, gems, evenings with Emma and the flights by night, no, not that again. Physique, too soon, perhaps never, vague bowed body bonewhite when light at full, nothing clear but ashen glare as imagined, no, attitudes too with play of joints most clear more various now. For nine and nine eighteen that is four feet and more across in which to kneel, arse on heels, hands on thighs, trunk best bowed and crown on ground. And even sit, knees drawn up, trunk best bowed, head between knees, arms round knees to hold all together. And even lie, arse to knees say diagonal ac, feet say at d, head on left cheek at b. Price to pay and highest lying more flesh touching glowing ground. But say not glowing enough to burn and turning over, see how that works. Arse to knees, say bd, feet say at c, head on right cheek at a. Then arse to knees say again ac, but feet at b and head on left cheek at d. Then arse to knees say again bd, but feet at a and head on right cheek at c. So on other four possibilities when begin again. All that most clear. Imaginable too flat on back, knees drawn up, hands holding shins to hold all together, glare on ceiling, whereas flat on face by no stretch. Place then most clear so far but of him nothing and perhaps never save jointed segments variously disposed white when light at full. And always there among them somewhere the glaring eyes now clearer still in that flashes of vision few and far now rive their unseeingness. So for example as chance may have it on the ceiling a flyspeck or the insect itself or a strand of Emma's motte. Then lost and all the remaining field for hours of time on earth.

Imagination dead imagine to lodge a second in that glare a dying common house or dying window fly, then fall the five feet to the dust and die and fall. No, no image, no fly here, no life or dying here but his, a speck of dirt. Or hers since sex not seen so far, say Emma standing, turning, sitting, kneeling, lying, in dark and light, saying to herself, She's not here, no sound, Fancy is her only hope, and Emmo on the walls, first the face, handsome beyond words, then deasil details later. And how crouching down and back she turns murmuring, Fancy her being all kissed, licked, sucked, fucked and so on by all that, no sound, hands on knees to hold herself together. Till halt and up, no, no image, down, for her down, to sit or kneel, kneel, arse on heels, hands on thighs, trunk bowed, breasts hanging, crown on ground, eyes glaring, no, no image, eyes closed, long lashes black when light, no more glare, never was, long black hair strewn when light, murmuring, no sound, Fancy dead. Any

length, in dark and light, then topple left,
arse to knees say db, feet say at c, head
on left cheek at a, left breast puckered in
the dust, hands, imagine hands. Imagine
hands. Let her lie so from now on, have
always lain so, head on left cheek in
black hair at a and the rest the only way,
never sat, never knelt, never stood, no
Emmo, no need, never was. Imagine
hands. Left on ball of right shoulder
holding enough not to slip, right lightly
clenched on ground, something in this
hand, imagine later, something soft,
clench tight, then lax and still any length,
then tight again, so on, imagine later.
Highest point from ground top to swell
of right haunch, say twenty inches, slim
woman. Ceiling wrong now, down two
foot, perfect cube now, three foot every
way, always was, light as before, all
bonewhite when at full as before, floor
like bleached dirt, something there, leave
it for the moment. Waste height, sixteen
inches, strange, say some reason unimaginable now, imagine later, imagination

dead imagine all strange away. Jolly and
Draeger gone, never were. So far then
hollow cube three foot overall, no way in
imagined yet, none out. Black cold any
length, then light slow up to full glare say
ten seconds still and hot glare any length
all ivory white all six planes no shadow,
then down through deepening greys and
gone, so on. Walls and ceiling flaking
plaster or suchlike, floor like bleached
dirt, aha, something there, leave it for the
moment. Call floor angles deasil a, b, c
and d and in here Emma lying on her left
side, arse to knees along diagonal db with
arse towards d and knees towards b
though neither at either because too
short and waste space here too some reason yet to be imagined. On left side then
arse to knees db and consequently arse to
crown along wall da though not flush because arse out with head on left cheek at
a and remaining segment knees to feet
along bc not flush because knees out with
feet at c. In dark and light. Slow fade of
ivory flesh when ebb ten seconds and

gone. Long black hair when light strewn
over face and adjacent floor. Uncover
right eye and cheekbone vivid white for
long black lashes when light. Say again
though no real image puckered tip of left
breast, leave right a mere name. Left
hand clinging to right shoulder ball, right
more faint loose fist on ground till fingers
tighten as though to squeeze, imagine
later, then loose again and still any
length, so on. Murmuring, no sound,
though say lips move with faint stir of
hair, whether none emitted or air too
rare, Fancy is her only hope, or, She's not
here, or, Fancy dead, suggesting moments of discouragement, imagine other
murmurs. In dark and light, no, dark
alone, say murmurs now in dark alone as
though in light all ears all six planes all
ears when shining whereas in dark un-
heard, this a well-known thing. And yet
no sound, well say a sound too faint for
mortal ear. Imagine other murmurs. So
great need of words not daring till at last
slow ebb ten seconds, too fast, thirty

now, great need not daring till at last
slow ebb thirty seconds on earth through
a thousand darkening greys till out and
incontinent, Fancy dead, for instance if
spirits low, no sound. But see how the
light dies down and from half down or
more slow up again to full and the words
down again that were trembling up, all
right, say mere delay, dark must be in the
end, say dark and light here equal in the
end that is when all done with dead
imagining and measures taken dark and
light seen equal in the end. And indeed
how stay of flow or ebb at any grey any
length and even on the very sill of black
any length till at last in and black and at
long last the murmur too faint for mortal
ear. But murmurs in long dark so long
that longing no but need for light as in
long light for dark murmurs sometimes
as great a space apart as from on earth a
winter to a summer day and coming on
that great silence, She's not here, for instance if in better spirits or, Fancy is her
only hope, too faint for mortal ear. And

other times to imagine other extreme so
hard on one another any order and sometimes when all spent if not assuaged a
second time in some quite different so
run together that a mere torrent of hope
and unhope mingled and submission
amounting to nothing, get all this clearer
later. Imagine other murmurs, Mother
mother, Mother in heaven, Mother of
God, God in heaven, combinations with
Christ and Jesus, other proper names in
great numbers say of loved ones for the
most part and cherished haunts, imagine
as needed, unsupported interjections, an-
cient Greek philosophers ejaculated with
place of origin when possible suggesting
pursuit of knowledge at some period,
completed propositions such as, She is
not here, the exception, imagine others,
This is not possible, there is one, and
here another of exceptional length, In a
hammock in the sun in here the name of
some bewitching site she lies sleeping.
But sudden gleam that whatever words
given to let fall soundless in the dark that

if no sound better none, all right, try
sound and if no better say quite speech-
less, imagine sound and not till then all
that black hair toss back into the corner
baring face as about to when this hap-
pened. Quite audible then now for her
and if other ears there with her in the
dark for them and if ears low down in the
wall at a for them a voice without meaning, hear that. Then further quite
expressionless, ohs and ahs copulate cold
and no more feeling apparently in hammock than in Jesus Christ Almighty. And
finally for the moment and then that face
the tailaway so common in untrained
speakers leaving sometimes in some
doubt such things as which Diogenes and
what fancy her only. Such then the sound
roughly and if no clearer so then all the
storm unspoken and the silence un-
broken unless sound of light and dark or
at the moments of change a sound of flow
thirty seconds till full then silence any
length till sound of ebb thirty seconds till
black then silence any length, that might

repay hearing and she hearing open then
her eyes to lightening or darkening greys
and not close them then to keep them
closed till next sound of change till full
light or dark, that might well be imagined. But at the same time say here all
sound most doubtful though still too
soon to deny and that in the end that is
when all gone from mind and all mind
gone that then none ever been but only
silent flesh unless with the faint rise and
fall of breast the breath to whip up to a
pant if too faint alone and all others de-
nied but still too soon. Hollow cube then
three foot overall, full glare, head on left
cheek in angle a and the rest the only
way and say though no clear image now
the long black hair now scattered clear of
face on floor so clear when strewn on
face now gone some reason, come back
to that later, and on the face now bare all
the glare for the moment. Gone the re-
membered long black lashes vivid white
so clear before through gap in hair before
all tossed back and lost some reason and

face quite bare suggesting perhaps confu-
sion then with errant threads of hair itself
confused then with long lashes and so
gone with hair or some other reason now
quite gone. Cease here from face a space
to note how place no longer cube but
rotunda three foot diameter eighteen inches high supporting a dome semi-
circular in section as in the Pantheon at
Rome or certain beehive tombs and consequently three foot from ground to
vertex that is at its highest point no lower
than before with loss of floor space in the
neighbourhood of two square feet or six
square inches per lost angle and conse-
quences for recumbent readily imaginable and of cubic an even higher figure, all
right, resume face. But a, b, c and d now
where any pair of right-angled diameters
meet circumference meaning tighter fit
for Emma with loss if folded as before of
nearly one foot from crown to arse and of
more than one from arse to knees and of
nearly one from knees to feet though she
still might be mathematically speaking

more than seven foot long and merely a
question of refolding in such a way that if
head on left cheek at new a and feet at
new c then arse no longer at new d but
somewhere between it and new c and
knees no longer at new b but somewhere
between it and new a with segments an-
gled more acutely that is head almost
touching knees and feet almost touching
arse, all that most clear. Rotunda then
three foot diameter and three from
ground to vertex, full glare, head on left
cheek at a no longer new, when suddenly
clear these dimensions faulty and small
woman scarce five foot fully extended
making rotunda two foot diameter and
two from ground to verge, full glare, face
on left cheek at a and long segment that
is from crown to arse now necessarily
along diagonal too hastily assigned to
middle with result face on left cheek with
crown against wall at a and no longer feet
but _arse_ against wall at c there being no
alternative and knees against wall ab a
few inches from face and feet against

wall bc a few inches from arse there
being no alternatives and in this way the
body tripled or trebled up and wedged in
the only possible way in one half of the
available room leaving the other empty,
aha.

DIAGRAM

Arms and hands as before for the moment. Rotunda then two foot across and
at its highest two foot high, full glare,
face on left cheek at a, long black hair
gone, long black lashes on white cheekbone gone, glare from above for features
on this bonewhite undoubted face right
profile still hungering for missing lashes
burning down for commissure of lids at
least when like say without hesitation
hell gaping they part and the black eye
appears, leave now this face for the moment. Glare now on hands most womanly clear and womanly especially right
still loosely clenched as before but no
longer on ground since corrected pose

but now on outer of right knee just where it swells to thigh while left still loosely hitched to right shoulder ball as before. All that most clear. That black eye still yawning before going down to former to see what all this squeezing note how the other slips a little way down slope of upper arm then back up to ball, imagine squeeze again. Loose clench any length then crush down most womanly straining knuckles five seconds then back lax any length, all right, now down while fingers loose and in between tips and palm that tiny chink, full glare all this time. No real image but say like red no grey say like something grey and when again squeeze firm down five seconds say faint hiss then silence then back loose two seconds and say faint pop and so arrive though no true image at small grey punctured rubber ball or small grey ordinary rubber bulb such as on earth attached to bottle of scent or suchlike that when squeezed a jet of scent but here alone. So little by little all strange away. Avalanche white

lava mud seethe lid over eye permitting
return to face of which finally only that it
could be nothing else, all right. Thence
on to neck in health by nature blank
chunk nearer to healthy natural neck
with even hint of jugular and cords suggesting perhaps past her best and thence
on down to other meat when suddenly
when least expected all this prying point-
less and enough for the moment and
perhaps for ever this place so clear now
when light at full and this body hinged
and crooked as only the human man or
woman living or not when light at full
without all this poking and prying about
for cracks holes and appendages. Rotunda then as before no change for the
moment in dark and light no visible
source spread even no shadow slow on
thirty seconds to full same off to black
two foot high at highest six and a half
round good measure, wall peeling plaster
or the like supporting dome semi-circular
in section same surface, floor bleached
dirt or similar, head wedged against wall

at a with blank face on left cheek and the
rest the only way that is arse wedged
against wall at c and knees wedged
against wall ab a few inches from face
and feet wedged against wall bc a few
inches from arse, puckered tip of left
breast no real image but maintain for the
moment, left hand most clear and womanly lightly clasping right shoulder ball
so lightly that slip from time to time
down slope of right upper arm then back
up to clasp, right no less on upper outer
right knee lightly clasping any length
small grey rubber sprayer bulb or grey
punctured rubber ball then squeeze five
seconds on earth faint hiss relax two seconds and pop or not, black right eye like
maintain hell gaping any length then
seethe of lid to cover imagine frequency
later and motive, left also at same time or
not or never imagine later, all contained
in one hemicycle leaving other vacant,
aha. All that if not yet quite complete
quite clear and little change likely unless
perhaps to complete unless perhaps

somehow light sudden gleam perhaps better fixed and all this flowing and ebbing to full and empty more harm than good and better unchanging black or glare one or the other or between the two soft white unchanging but leave for the moment as seen from outset and never doubted slow on and off thirty seconds to glare and black any length through slow lightening and darkening greys from nothing for no reason yet imagined. Sleep stirring now some time add now with nightmares unimaginable making waking sweet and lying waking till longing for sleep again with dread of demons, perhaps some glimpse of demons later. Dread then in rotunda now with longing and sweet relief but so faint and weak no more than weak tremors of a hothouse leaf. Memories of past felicity no save one faint with faint ripple of sorrow of a lying side by side, look at this closer later. Imagine turning over with help of hinge of neck to bow head towards breast and so temporarily shorten long segment

unwedging crown and arse with play
enough to writhe till finally head wedged
against wall at a as before but on right
cheek and arse against wall at c as before
but on right cheek and knees against wall
a few inches from face as before but wall
ad and feet against wall a few inches
from arse as before but wall cd and so all
tripled up and wedged as before but on
the other side to rest the other and within
the other hemicycle leaving the other vacant, aha, all that most clear. Clear
further how at some earlier more callow
stage this writhe again and again in vain
through weakness or natural awkward-
ness or want of pliancy or want of
resolution and how halfway through on
back with legs just clear how after some
time in the balance thus the fall back to
where she lay head wedged against wall
at a with blank face on left cheek and
arse against wall at c and knees against
wall ab and feet against wall bc with left
hand clutching lightly right shoulder ball
and right on upper outer knee small grey

sprayer bulb or grey punctured rubber ball with disappointment naturally tinged perhaps with relief and this again and again till final renouncement with faint sweet relief, faint disappointment will have been here too. Sleep if maintained with cacodemons making waking in light and dark if this maintained faint sweet relief and the longing for it again and to be gone again a folly to be resisted again in vain. No memories of felicity save with faint ruffle of sorrow of a lying side by side and of misfortune none, look closer later. So in rotunda up to now with disappointment and relief with dread and longing sorrow all so weak and faint no more than faint tremors of a leaf indoors on earth in winter to survive till spring. Glare back now where all no light immeasurable turmoil no sound black soundless storm of which on earth all being well say one millionth stilled to mean and of that as much again by the more fortunate all being well vented as only humans can. All gone now and

never been never stilled never voiced all
back whence never sundered unstillable
turmoil no sound, She's not here, Fancy
is her only, Mother mother, Mother in
heaven and of God, God in heaven,
Christ and Jesus all combinations, loved
ones and places, philosophers and all
mere cries, In a hammock etc. and all
such, leaving only for the moment, Fancy
dead, try that again with spirant barely
parting lips in murmur and faint stir of
white dust or not in light and dark if this
maintained or dark alone as though ears
when shining and dead uncertain in
dying fall of amateur soliloquy when not
known for certain. Last look oh not
farewell but last for now on right side
tripled up and wedged in half the room
head against wall at a and arse against
wall at c and knees against wall ab an
inch or so from head and feet against
wall bc an inch or so from arse. Then
look away then back for left hand clasping lightly right shoulder ball any length
till slip and back to clasp and right on

upper outer knee any length grey sprayer
bulb or small grey punctured rubber ball
till squeeze with hiss and loose again
with pop or not. Long black hair and
lashes gone and puckered breast no details to add to these for the moment save
normal neck with hint of cords and jugular and black bottomless eye. Within
apart from fancy dead and with faint sorrow faint memory of a lying side by side
and in sleep demons not yet imagined all
dark unappeasable turmoil no sound and
so exhaled only for the moment with
faint sound, Fancy dead, to which now
add for old mind's sake sorrow vented in
simple sighing sound black vowel a and
further so that henceforth here no other
sounds than these say gone now and
never were sprayer bulb or punctured
rubber ball and nothing ever in that hand
lightly closed on nothing any length till
for no reason yet imagined fingers
tighten then relax no sound and to the
same end slip of left hand down slope of
right upper arm no sound and same pur-

pose none of breath to the end that here
henceforth no other sounds than these
and never were that is than sop to mind
faint sighing sound for tremor of sorrow
at faint memory of a lying side by side
and fancy murmured dead.

A Piece
of Monologue

Curtain.

Faint diffuse light.

Speaker stands well off centre downstage audience left.

White hair, white nightgown, white socks.

Two metres to his left, same level, same height, standard lamp, skull-sized white globe, faintly lit.

Just visible extreme right, same level, white foot of pallet bed.

Ten seconds before speech begins.

Thirty seconds before end of speech lamplight begins to fail.

Lamp out. Silence. Speaker, globe, foot of pallet, barely visible in diffuse light.

Ten seconds.

Curtain.

SPEAKER: Birth was the death of him.
Again. Words are few. Dying too. Birth
was the death of him. Ghastly grinning
ever since. Up at the lid to come. In cra-
dle and crib. At suck first fiasco. With the
first totters. From mammy to nanny and
back. All the way. Bandied back and
forth. So ghastly grinning on. From funeral to funeral. To now. This night. Two
and a half billion seconds. Again. Two
and a half billion seconds. Hard to be-
lieve so few. From funeral to funeral.
Funerals of . . . he all but said of loved
ones. Thirty thousand nights. Hard to be-
lieve so few. Born dead of night. Sun long
sunk behind the larches. New needles
turning green. In the room dark gaining.
Till faint light from standard lamp. Wick
turned low. And now. This night. Up at
nightfall. Every nightfall. Faint light in
room. Whence unknown. None from
window. No. Next to none. No such thing

as none. Gropes to window and stares
out. Stands there staring out. Stock still
staring out. Nothing stirring in that black
vast. Gropes back in the end to where the
lamp is standing. Was standing. When
last went out. Loose matches in right-
hand pocket. Strikes one on his buttock
the way his father taught him. Takes off
milkwhite globe and sets it down. Match
goes out. Strikes a second as before.
Takes off chimney. Smoke-clouded.
Holds it in left hand. Match goes out.
Strikes a third as before and sets it to
wick. Puts back chimney. Match goes
out. Puts back globe. Turns wick low.
Backs away to edge of light and turns to
face east. Blank wall. So nightly. Up.
Socks. Nightgown. Window. Lamp.
Backs away to edge of light and stands
facing blank wall. Covered with pictures
once. Pictures of . . . he all but said of
loved ones. Unframed. Unglazed. Pinned
to wall with drawing-pins. All shapes and
sizes. Down one after another. Gone.
Torn to shreds and scattered. Strewn all

over the floor. Not at one sweep. No sudden fit of . . . no word. Ripped from the wall and torn to shreds one by one. Over the years. Years of night. Nothing on the wall now but the pins. Not all. Some out with the wrench. Some still pinning a shred. So stands there facing blank wall. Dying on. No more no less. No. Less. Less to die. Ever less. Like light at nightfall. Stands there facing east. Blank pinpocked surface once white in shadow. Could once name them all. There was father. That grey void. There mother. That other. There together. Smiling. Wedding day. There all three. That grey blot. There alone. He alone. Not now. Forgotten. All gone so long. Gone. Ripped off and torn to shreds. Scattered all over the floor. Swept out of the way under the bed and left. Thousand shreds under the bed with the dust and spiders. All the . . . he all but said the loved ones. Stands there facing the wall staring beyond. Nothing there either. Nothing stirring there either. Nothing stirring

anywhere. Nothing to be seen anywhere.
Nothing to be heard anywhere. Room
once full of sounds. Faint sounds.
Whence unknown. Fewer and fainter as
time wore on. Nights wore on. None
now. No. No such thing as none. Rain
some nights still slant against the panes.
Or dropping gentle on the place beneath.
Even now. Lamp smoking though wick
turned low. Strange. Faint smoke issuing
through vent in globe. Low ceiling
stained by night after night of this. Dark
shapeless blot on surface elsewhere
white. Once white. Stands facing wall
after the various motions described. That
is up at nightfall and into gown and
socks. No. In them already. In them all
night. All day. All day and night. Up at
nightfall in gown and socks and after a
moment to get his bearings gropes to
window. Faint light in room. Unutterably
faint. Whence unknown. Stands stock
still staring out. Into black vast. Nothing
there. Nothing stirring. That he can see.
Hear. Dwells thus as if unable to move

again. Or no will left to move again. Not
enough will left to move again. Turns in
the end and gropes to where he knows
the lamp is standing. Thinks he knows.
Was last standing. When last went out.
Match one as described for globe. Two
for chimney. Three for wick. Chimney
and globe back on. Turns wick low.
Backs away to edge of light and turns to
face wall. East. Still as the lamp by his
side. Gown and socks white to take faint
light. Once white. Hair white to take faint
light. Foot of pallet just visible edge of
frame. Once white to take faint light.
Stands there staring beyond. Nothing.
Empty dark. Till first word always the
same. Night after night the same. Birth.
Then slow fade up of a faint form. Out of
the dark. A window. Looking west. Sun
long sunk behind the larches. Light
dying. Soon none left to die. No. No such
thing as no light. Starless moonless
heaven. Dies on to dawn and never dies.
There in the dark that window. Night
slowly falling. Eyes to the small pane

gaze at that first night. Turn from it in the
end to face the darkened room. There in
the end slowly a faint hand. Holding aloft
a lighted spill. In light of spill faintly the
hand and milkwhite globe. Then second
hand. In light of spill. Takes off globe and
disappears. Reappears empty. Takes off
chimney. Two hands and chimney in
light of spill. Spill to wick. Chimney back
on. Hand with spill disappears. Second
hand disappears. Chimney alone in
gloom. Hand reappears with globe.
Globe back on. Turns wick low. Pale
globe alone in gloom. Glimmer of brass
bedrail. Fade. Birth the death of him.
That nevoid smile. Thirty thousand
nights. Stands at edge of lamplight staring beyond. Into dark whole again.
Window gone. Hands gone. Light gone.
Gone. Again and again. Again and again
gone. Till dark slowly parts again. Grey
light. Rain pelting. Umbrellas round a
grave. Seen from above. Streaming black
canopies. Black ditch beneath. Rain bubbling in the black mud. Empty for the

moment. That place beneath. Which . . .
he all but said which loved one? Thirty
seconds. To add to the two and a half
billion odd. Then fade. Dark whole
again. Blest dark. No. No such thing as
whole. Stands staring beyond half hearing what he's saying. He? The words
falling from his mouth. Making do with
his mouth. Lights lamp as described.
Backs away to edge of light and turns to
face wall. Stares beyond into dark. Waits
for first word always the same. It gathers
in his mouth. Parts lips and thrusts
tongue forward. Birth. Parts the dark.
Slowly the window. That first night. The
room. The spill. The hands. The lamp.
The gleam of brass. Fade. Gone. Again
and again gone. Mouth agape. A cry. Sti-
fled by nasal. Dark parts. Grey light. Rain
pelting. Streaming umbrellas. Ditch.
Bubbling black mud. Coffin out of frame.
Whose? Fade. Gone. Move on to other
matters. Try to move on. To other matters. How far from wall? Head almost
touching. As at window. Eyes glued to

pane staring out. Nothing stirring. Black vast. Stands there stock still staring out as if unable to move again. Or gone the will to move again. Gone. Faint cry in his ear. Mouth agape. Closed with hiss of breath. Lips joined. Feel soft touch of lip on lip. Lip lipping lip. Then parted by cry as before. Where is he now? Back at window staring out. Eyes glued to pane. As if looking his last. Turns away at last and gropes through faint unaccountable light to unseen lamp. White gown moving through that gloom. Once white. Lights and moves to face wall as described. Head almost touching. Stands there staring beyond waiting for first word. It gathers in his mouth. Parts lips and thrusts tongue between them. Tip of tongue. Feel soft touch of tongue on lips. Of lips on tongue. Stare beyond through rift in dark to other dark. Further dark. Sun long sunk behind the larches. Nothing stirring. Nothing faintly stirring. Stock still eyes glued to pane. As if looking his last. At that first night. Of thirty

thousand odd. Where soon to be. This
night to be. Spill. Hands. Lamp. Gleam of
brass. Pale globe alone in gloom. Brass
bedrail catching light. Thirty seconds. To
swell the two and a half billion odd. Fade.
Gone. Cry. Snuffed with breath of
nostrils. Again and again. Again and
again gone. Till whose grave? Which . . .
he all but said which loved one's? He?
Black ditch in pelting rain. Way out
through the grey rift in dark. Seen from
on high. Streaming canopies. Bubbling
black mud. Coffin on its way. Loved one
. . . he all but said loved one on his way.
Her way. Thirty seconds. Fade. Gone.
Stands there staring beyond. Into dark
whole again. No. No such thing as whole.
Head almost touching wall. White hair
catching light. White gown. White socks.
White foot of pallet edge of frame stage
left. Once white. Least . . . give and head
rests on wall. But no. Stock still head
haught staring beyond. Nothing stirring.
Faintly stirring. Thirty thousand nights of
ghosts beyond. Beyond that black be-

yond. Ghost light. Ghost nights. Ghost rooms. Ghost graves. Ghost . . . he all but said ghost loved ones. Waiting on the rip word. Stands there staring beyond at that black veil lips quivering to half-heard words. Treating of other matters. Trying to treat of other matters. Till half hears there are no other matters. Never were other matters. Never two matters. Never but the one matter. The dead and gone. The dying and the going. From the word go. The word begone. Such as the light going now. Beginning to go. In the room. Where else? Unnoticed by him staring beyond. The globe alone. Not the other. The unaccountable. From nowhere. On all sides nowhere. The globe alone. Alone gone.